Growing God's Way

Stories and Songs of the 5 Solas

Stories by Grace Chung
Illustrations by Cami Ferreira

JUBAL HOUSE

semper reformanda

FIVE SOLAS PROJECT

Through the centuries, theologians and pastors have encouraged and challenged Christians to grow in their faith with the call of "**semper reformanda**," literally meaning "always reforming." One writer states that we are "always in need of being reformed according to the Word of God."

This call for continuous growth in faith blends with the Five Sola themes that emerged since the 16th century. These five themes represent a set of key beliefs that provide a foundational focus for an active, growing life of faith in God: **scripture alone** (2 Tim. 3:16-17), **faith alone** (Rom. 5:1), **grace alone** (Eph. 2:8), **Christ alone** (Gal. 2:16), and **the glory of God alone** (1 Cor. 10:31).

In this story book and the accompanying songs, the writer, illustrator, and composer have brought to life each of the Five Solas for children of all ages. It is our prayer that these stories and songs will encourage each reader and listener to creatively meditate more deeply on God, and in so doing, live out a dynamically growing, ever-changing, and deeper faith: "semper reformanda."

GROWING GOD'S WAY: STORIES AND SONGS OF THE 5 SOLAS

Edited by Mary Lou Willmington & Nicolette Kay
Book and CD Design by Gus Ferreira

Published by Jubal House
135 N. Oakland Ave.
Pasadena, CA 91182

JUBAL HOUSE is a registered trademark of the Fred Bock Institute of Music

ISBN: 978-1-934596-07-4 (paperback w/ CD – sold only as a set)

Library of Congress Control Number: 2016950634

Printed in the USA

TABLE OF CONTENTS

Seeds of Faith

There once was a girl who loved to plant seeds,
To allow them to flourish and use them for good deeds.
She would dig up the dirt in her small space outside,
And lovingly drop in the kernels with pride.

But the winters were dry and the summers were hot.
We really need the rain, the little girl thought.
Grandma loves her roses, and Grandpa loves his beans;
Mama loves her sunflowers and Papa his leafy greens!

So the little girl prayed and asked for the rain
That all her work might not be in vain.
She waited and waited, knowing God would hear her call.
But no drizzle, no snowfall, no nothing at all.

"I know God can hear me. He knows what I need.
If only I keep believing with the faith of a mustard seed.
My God can do all things so great and so small.
He will send the rain and make my plants grow tall."

With knit cap and rain coat, booted and gloved,
She prayed as she circled the garden she loved.
Like Joshua marching around Jericho city,
The little girl showed herself to be nothing but gritty.

A week went by, day after day,
And all she could do was continue to pray.
When others would tell her to just give it up,
She simply responded, "I will not give up!"

Two weeks went by, day after day,
And still the little girl continued to pray.
"Dear God, right now there's not a cloud in the sky.
But still I will not let my faith run dry."

Three weeks went by, day after day.
Determined as ever, the little girl continued to pray.
"Where is the rain, God? I don't know why.
My plants are dying…they need You to cry!"

The fourth week arrived
and early one morning,
Thunder and lightning came
without any warning!
Within minutes the skies darkened
and clouds gathered 'round,
Then raindrops fell heavily
and landed on the ground.

Squealing and laughing and shrieking with delight,
The little girl bounced all around almost giving
her parents a fright!
"I knew it would come, I knew it would rain!
My flowers and plants are no longer in pain!"

With a smile so big it could cover the earth,
The little girl realized what her belief was worth.
"My faith is in You, Creator, Almighty One.
Thank You, Father, Spirit, Son."

Growing in Christ

"Come, children, it's time for worship!" Grandma called out to the little ones who were washed, dressed in their pajamas, and ready for bed.

"Now," Grandma said, "tonight we are going to talk about getting to heaven. Don't you all want to go to heaven?" "Yes!" they all cried out. "We want to go to heaven to see Jesus!"

"So how do we get to heaven?" she asked. For a moment, there was silence.

Then, AJ spoke up. "We have to become big and strong like my bear," he said, as he held up his favorite stuffed animal. "I think God wants us to be tough so that we can help the weaker people stand up to the bad people."

Alexa also answered. "We need to be sweet and gentle like my lamb," she said, hugging her favorite stuffed animal. "I think God wants us to be kind so that we can help people feel loved and accepted."

"Or be happy and cheerful like my mouse!" exclaimed Zoey, showing off her favorite stuffed animal. "I think God wants us to be joyful so that we can help people forget about their worries and sadness."

"Yes, those are all good things," Grandma replied. "And what about you, Carter?" she asked the little one.

Carter looked up, squeezing her favorite stuffed doll, Sweet Pea, and said with a big grin on her face, "We should be tasty like sweet peas!"

Grandma laughed and smiled at all her grandkids. Then she picked up her Bible and opened it to the book of John, reading: " 'Jesus said...,"I am the way, and the truth, and the life. No one comes to the Father except through me." '

"So in order to get to heaven, we have to get to know Jesus. In order to get to know Jesus, we have to read our Bibles. The Bible tells about Jesus and His love for us. He cares for us so much that He died on the cross for our sins. If we ask Jesus to forgive us of our sins, come into our hearts, and be the Lord of our lives, then someday we can be in heaven with Him. Isn't that such a wonderful act of love?"

Grandma looked around at their curious faces.

"So yes, AJ, we should be big and strong to help those who need our help. And yes, Alexa, we should be gentle and kind to make people feel loved. And we should be cheerful, like Zoey said. And who doesn't love being tasty like sweet peas?" she said, as she winked at Carter.

"But we should be all those things because that's what Jesus was like; and as we get to know Jesus, we will want to become more like Him in every way."

Thinking about what their grandma had just said, they all crawled into bed and said their prayers, asking to know and be more like Jesus. Grandma tucked them all in and gave each a big kiss.

"Sweet pea dreams," she said softly, as she turned out the lights and quietly left the room.

Garden of Grace

"In the beginning, God rested." Christian and Joshua looked up in surprise, as their dad read from the Bible. "What did you say?" Joshua asked.

"On the first day, God rested. He needed to gather up His energy so that He could create the world during the rest of the week."

"No, I don't think that's right," Christian said, as he reached for the Bible. He had heard the Creation story many times before, and that was not how he remembered it starting. "Turn to Genesis 1, Christian!" said Joshua. "It's at the beginning of the Bible!"

But Dad continued, "On day two, God created a man and a woman, and He called them Adam and Eve. He also created all the creepy, crawly creatures of the earth."

Now the boys KNEW that this was wrong. "What if He made us and there was no land and light?" Christian asked. "We would be in the dark water drowning!"

But this got them thinking. What if God had made humans first? What if He created everything backwards? Then what would have happened during the rest of the week?

If there was no land and no light, Adam, Eve, and the animals would have been floating around in the darkness, not knowing what the others looked like.

They might have bumped into a rhinoceros with its large horn, an elephant with its curvy long trunk, or maybe even a porcupine with its prickly quills!

Then God would have created great whales and other creatures of the sea. All the animals would be sloshing around in the waters, being tossed and turned in every direction.

He also would have made the birds that fly above the earth. But without the light, eagles, hummingbirds, and even owls would bump into each other wherever they went. Maybe only the bats would have liked it!

On the fourth day, God would have finally created some light! The sun, moon, and stars would have appeared so that the winged creatures no longer flew right into each other.

Adam would have finally seen what Eve looked like, and they both would have finally seen the porcupine that might have poked them in the ocean.

Only then would God have brought the earth from out of the water so that Adam, Eve, and all the creepy, crawly creatures could walk on land.

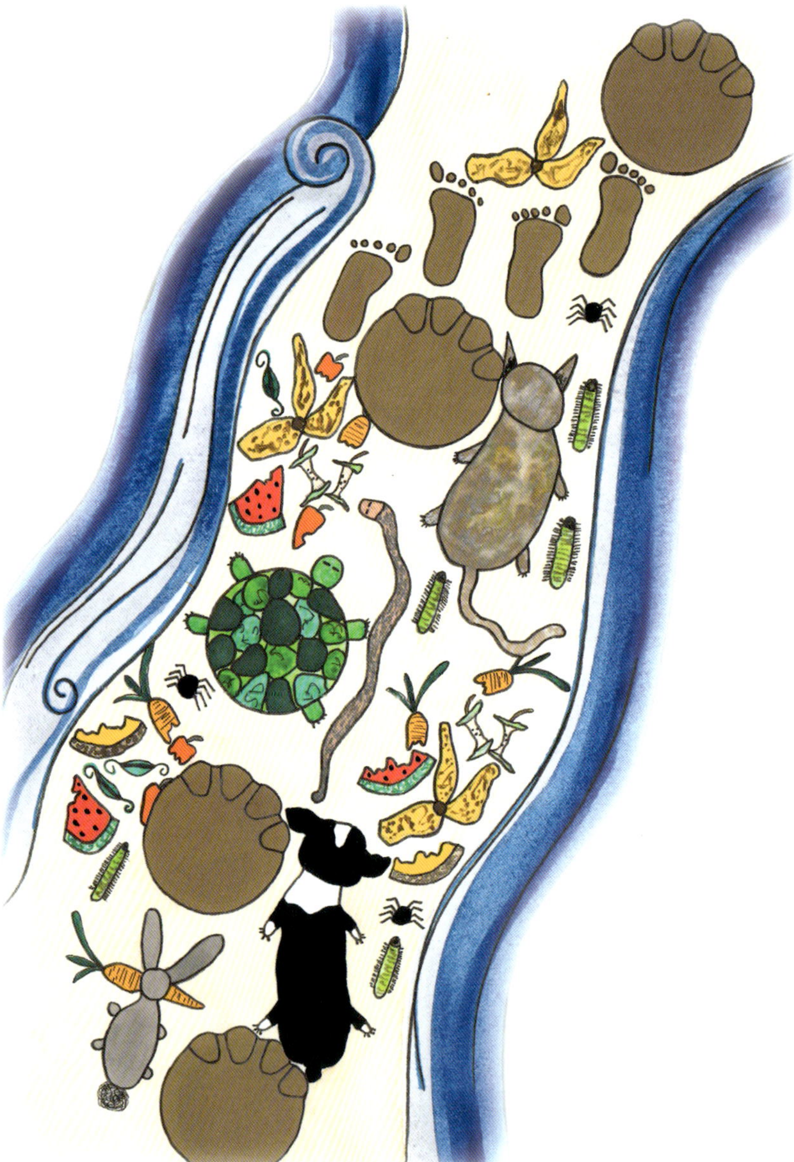

The planting of fruit trees and vegetables would also have allowed them to eat. And oh, how hungry they would have been! They wouldn't have eaten for three days!

Then, on the next day, what if God decided to separate the waters of Heaven from the waters of Earth? Adam and Eve would have witnessed something very peculiar. They would have seen water coming up from the seas and floating up towards the sky!

After all of that would have come evening and morning, which God called Night and Day. Finally, the week would have been over. But how tired every creature would be!

"So," Dad asked, "what are you most thankful for about creation?" Christian sat back and thought for a moment.

Then he answered, "God's grace. He was so smart because He made us last. God knew the right order. I'm thankful He made us last."

Rooted in Scripture

Look beyond the stories, and what do you see?
It's a letter from our Creator, asking us to know Him,
and enter into our lives.

But God sends us
this message from above
to illustrate His character
and **love.**

Look beyond the story of Adam and Eve.
They ate the fruit from the tree of
knowledge of good and evil,
and sin entered into their lives.

But God created a plan of
salvation
to give us another chance.

Look beyond the struggles of Abraham and Sarah.
They had given up on the hope of having children,
and doubt entered into their lives.

But God
gave them a **promise**

of future generations they couldn't even imagine.

Look beyond the trials of Joseph.
He was sold as a slave by his own brothers,
and sadness entered into his life.

But God used him to
save
a nation from hunger and
starvation.

Look beyond the frustrations of Moses.
He led the Israelites out of slavery,
and yet complaining entered into his life.

But God used him to **lead**

His children toward the land of milk and honey.

Look beyond the battles of David.
He had only ever been a shepherd,
and Goliath entered into his life.

But God made his slingshot
and five little stones
bring down
the towering giant.

Look beyond the beauty of Esther.
The jealousy of a power-hungry Haman threatened her people's lives,
and fear entered into her life.

But God used her to gain favor with the king and **protect** her people from harm.

Look beyond the baptisms of John.
He spent his life preparing the way for Jesus,
and still tribulations entered into his life.

But God showed that even prison would not defeat the message of His **faithful** disciple.

Look beyond the flaws of the apostles.
They gave up everything to follow their Master and, in the end, ridicule and persecution entered into their lives.

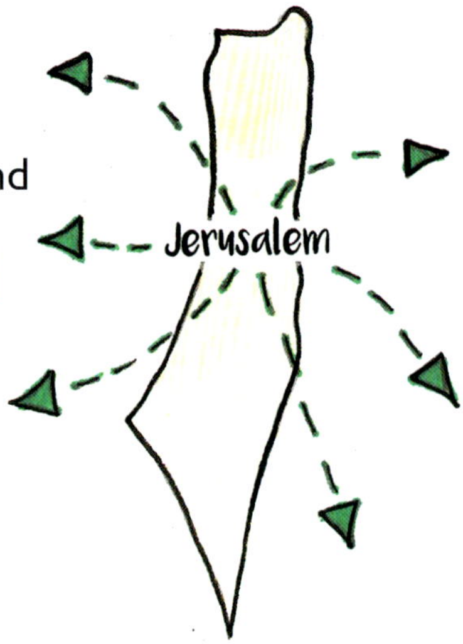

But God saw their faithfulness and blessed their **ministry** even after the cross.

Look beyond the denials of Peter.
He rejected His Lord three times, and unbearable guilt entered into his life.

But God built the **church** upon his leadership.

Look beyond the temptations of Jesus.
He suffered and died on the
cross for our sins
when the weight of the world
entered into His life.

But God proved that His Son is the **King**
and the **Savior**
when He rose from the dead.

Look beyond the stories, and what do you see?
It's a letter from our Creator, asking us to know Him,
and enter into our lives.

Because God sent us
His message from above
as an illustration
of His character and
love.

Blossoming in God's Glory

It was a beautiful summer day, and Florence was going to visit the zoo for the very first time. As she entered the gates, her mouth opened in awe as she saw all the exotic animals surrounded by nature.

Turning to her parents, she asked, "Can I explore the zoo with my guardian angel today?" Her parents were a bit surprised at the request but agreed to give her space and walk a few paces behind her.

"Angel," Florence said, "come. Will you tell me of the wonders that God created?" And so they began their day of exploration.

Their first point of arrival was at a fence overlooking a lion's lair. "Angel, will you tell me about the lions?"

The angel smiled and replied, "These are the ferocious animals that were placed in a den with Daniel. But because God was protecting His faithful servant, the lions did not attack. Instead, they bowed to the glory and majesty of the Protector of all."

"How frightening!" said Florence. "But how wonderful it is to have God watching over us!"

They continued along towards the aquarium, and upon entering Florence said, "Angel, will you tell me about the great fish of the ocean?"

The angel replied, "This is the great creature that swallowed Jonah when he was thrown into the raging sea. God was teaching His servant a lesson, and after spitting Jonah back out onto land, the great fish bowed to the glory and majesty of the wisest Teacher of all."

"Oh, how that must have smelled," said Florence, as she scrunched her nose. "But how wonderful it is to have a God that gives us a second chance."

They exited the aquarium and walked towards the aviary. "Angel, will you tell me about the birds?"

The angel replied, "These are the messengers of the sky that searched for dry land after the great flood. God was guiding them so that Noah and his family would soon be safely back on the earth. When it was time, the dove left, bowing to the glory and majesty of the One who shows us the way."

"That must have been a long time in the big ark!" said Florence, as she thought of all that rocking back and forth. "But how wonderful it is to have God to guide us in the right direction."

The final place they arrived at was a barn. "Angel, will you tell me about the sheep and the donkeys?"

The angel replied,"These are the lowly animals that were present at the birth of Christ many, many years ago. On that night, in the stable, they bowed to the glory and majesty of the newborn King."

What lucky creatures, thought Florence. How wonderful it must have been to witness such an amazing thing!

As the day at the zoo came to a close, Florence and her parents got ready for the trip back home.

"How did you enjoy your day?" her mother asked. "What did you learn?"

Florence replied excitedly, "It was lovely! I learned that even the birds of the sky and the creatures of the ocean bow to the glory and majesty of God! How wonderful it is to know that the God who created you and me created all these beautiful animals to show us just how much He cares for us."

"I'm so glad you had a good day," her mother responded. Turning to the seat next to her, Florence whispered, "Thank you, angel, for teaching me about the glory of God." Then she closed her eyes, content, as they headed home.

Grace Chung is a musician, composer, and author. She maintains an active performance career and has had the privilege of sharing her music across the United States, Europe, and South America. In addition to authoring *Growing God's Way*, Grace has arranged a set of hymns for organ under the title *Jesus Loves Me*, in collaboration with the Brehm New Music Initiative. She plans to continue in her creative pursuits, as well as finding new and innovative ways for audiences to connect with the arts.

Cami Ferreira attended Arizona State University, where she earned a BFA in Photography. She then studied at the Fashion Institute of Design and Merchandising, where she received a degree in Fashion Design. Cami has been interested in writing and illustrating children's books since she was a child and is currently creating her own children's book series. She uses real materials, mostly brush-painted liquid watercolor and gouache, along with illustration markers. Cami lives in southern California with her husband and two kids, where she drives an awesome mini-van and loves to sing.